How To Be Rich

Discover How To Be Rich Using Money Rules Of The Rich To Make Money, Gain Passive Income, Be Debt Free, And Financially Free In 6 Simple Steps!

James Harper

STOP!!! Before you read any further....Would you like to know the Success Secrets of how to make Passive Income Online?

If your answer is yes, then you are not alone. Thousands of people are looking for the secret to learning how to create their own online passive income style business.

If you have been searching for these answers without much luck, you are in the right place!

Because I want to make sure to give you as much value as possible for purchasing this book, right now for a limited time you can get 3 incredible bonuses for free.

At the end of this book I describe all 3 bonuses. You can access them at the end. But for those of you that want to grab your bonuses right now. See below.

Just Go Here For Free Instant Access:

www.OperationAwesomeLife.com/FreeBonuses

Legal Notice

Disclaimer Notice

Table Of Contents

Introduction

I want to thank you and congratulate you for purchasing the book, *"How To Be Rich - Discover How To Be Rich Using Money Rules Of The Rich To Make Money, Gain Passive Income, Be Debt Free, And Financially Free In 6 Simple Steps!"*.

This book contains proven steps and strategies on how to think and operate your financial affairs like the wealthy.

Have you ever wondered how you can take two people working the same job with the same salary and one seems to always have money while the other seems to always be broke? Or have you ever wondered how a self made millionaire is able to rise out of the lower level of society while another seems to be trapped?

Well, if you have ever contemplated on these things, then you are in the right place! There is a process to wealth creation, some may call it a formula, but it is undoubtedly not the result of luck. If you want to get from A-Z, if you want to get to the top of the mountain, you have to have a roadmap. This is your roadmap.

Sometimes the hardest thing to do is to start! Unfortunately this is also the most important part. If you never start, you will never accomplish anything in life, let alone major ambitions. Please don't delay any longer! Stop putting your future on hold, and begin at once towards the amazing life you were born to live and should already be enjoying! I wish you the best of luck in this endeavor, and hope you will choose this book and its principles to be a part of your exciting accent to the top!

Thanks again for purchasing this book, I hope you enjoy it!

Chapter 1 - Living Within 80% Or Less Of Your Income

The fact that you have an income doesn't mean that you need to spend all those income as you please. Sure you can – but you should not if you want to become rich. Many people believe that they work to live and vice versa, thus making them slaves of the vicious cycle of "working for a living". This need not happen to you, and it certainly would not if you follow the rules on accumulating wealth.

The first thing that you need to remember is that you should live within 80% or less of your income. Yes, you heard it right! You cannot go all out with your pay check if you want to become rich. The next question would be: what would you do with your money?

As a basic rule, you need some part of your income to be able to afford your basic needs, i.e. water, food, clothes, electricity etc. You simply have to, or you will not survive. The good news is that there is no problem with spending on them so long as you put a limit on how much you need to spend. You see, being rich does not mean that you have to deprive yourself of the things you need. After all, you have worked hard for that money and you deserve to have a piece of it.

In spending the money you have earned, make sure that you don't go beyond the allowable limit which is 80%. Remember that the 80% should answer for all the things you need to buy or pay for. This goes to tell that you should not have expenses beyond the 80% limit. If you are earning $1200 per month, make sure that your way of living can be sustained by $960 per month and no more. This should cover your food, water and electric bills, rent (if any), transportation costs, and other expenses. If the $960 is not enough for you to last a month, you need to cut off on expenses that you don't need i.e. movie 3x/month, VIP golf membership dues, etc. In simple words, cut those expenses that would go beyond your limit.

You may ask, "Why do I need to do that when the entire $1200 can cover all that?" The answer is simple – because you want to be rich. How does spending on 80% of your income make you rich? Here's how:

- It puts a limit on spending

Since you have a ceiling on your allowable expenses, it automatically shuts off further spending on your part. The fact that you are only allowed to spend on a certain extent makes you think about *not spending* the rest, hence a spending limit you would not otherwise have.

- It helps you to determine which ones you really need

People often buy things they don't really need, resulting both wasted time and money. But because you are only allowed to spend 80% of your income, you are now forced to determine which ones are among the priority expenses. As such, you will have to dispense with the things you don't really need to prevent wasted resources and focus on the more important things that you need in your life.

- It allows you to have spare money

Spare money is very important in maintaining one's financial stability. Life is very uncertain and more often than not, people won't really have time to prepare for the next expenses to come. Saving 20% of your income helps you to gain some leverage financially, especially in times of need.

- It hones your skill of managing your finances

Some say that people show their ability and discipline best when confronted with boundaries or limitations. Having an 80% spending limit tests your skill in managing your finances, which in turn could hone you to become a better and wiser spender in the long run.

Now that you know what to do with 80% of your income, the next thing that you have to know is what to do with the remaining 20%. What does that 20% represent? How does that 20% make a difference in your way of life?

The remaining 20% of your income represents your savings. It is the spare money that you can count on in times of need, thus giving you some financial security and room for other necessary expenses. It gives you more power financially and more security psychologically because you won't be threatened by life events you never planned or in any way expected. In other words, you would be more economically stable. Such amount can make a huge difference between financial uncertainty and financial stability. Of course you wouldn't want to be on the bad side, would you?

However, do not be too complacent with the fact that you have saved at least 20% of your income in a storage box. The fact is, the way you manage that 20% savings is as important as the way you manage the 80% of your income. If you want to be rich, there is no question that you should manage both WISELY. But exactly how can you do that?

Here are where your savings should go:

- Business Fund

  As you will learn later on, having a business investment is very important in creating wealth. Surely, you would need a capital from which you would build your business. Save a business fund for this goal as early as today so that you will have enough money when the time comes that you are ready to venture into the business world.

- Charity Fund

    Set aside being filthy rich – what you need to be is a rich man with a heart. As a person, you need to help people in need whether they are complete strangers or the closest of your friends. As the law of karma always says, helping is an investment in itself. Surely, you want to reap the fruits of your good deeds later on!

- Emergency Fund

    No one knows for sure what will happen next. The future is uncertain and the only way for you to be prepared for what might come is to make sure that your weapons are ready. Have an emergency fund that you can count on anytime and in any event so you won't be caught off guard!

- Car Fund

    A means of transportation is also very essential in building your wealth. In order to be rich, you need to have the ability to move around places as you deal with transactions. This could only be attained by having a reliable means of transport – a car.

    This car fund is not only to be used to purchase a car (if you don't have one yet); it should also be a fund ready to answer for car repairs and improvements.

- Miscellaneous Fund

    Expenses which cannot be classified into a specified group should be covered under miscellaneous fund. This is where you should get the money to finance unexpected, little costs you haven't expected in your budget. This gives you a little leeway for spending on things that you need but failed to account for in your budget.

- Pleasure Fund

    Truth be told, pleasure is a basic human need. Whether it is as grand as having a world cruise or a simple movie per week agenda, your pleasure has to be incorporated in your life.

    All people have their own choices when it comes to what gives them pleasure, some more costly than others. The reason why you need to have a fund to answer for your pleasure expenses is so that you will never have to choose or compromise between necessities and pleasure. You can have both and still be rich! You might think that these funds cannot be covered by the 20% fund alone, and you're correct about that to an extent. But the thing is, these are some of the funds that you can utilize in times of need.

The manner on which you want to distribute the savings is up to you; you may divide the 20% equally or depending on your priorities. If you badly want a car, you may allot more to your car fund that in any other funds. You see, there is no hard and fast rule when it comes to your savings so long as you have these important fund classifications with you. All of these accounts are important for you to attain the financial stability you're aiming for.

To better utilize these funds, you can go to a reliable credit union where you can set up 6 accounts representing each fund. Aside from having them take care of your accounts of you, you can also be sure that you won't be able to spend your money on impulse as when you have the money on hand.

If you don't find (or want) a credit union to handle your savings, you can definitely just use an envelope to separate these funds under one account. Either way, you accomplish your goal of savings utilization by putting up different funds.

Chapter 2 – Make Wise Investments

After knowing the most important step in amassing wealth, you are now about to learn about the steps you actually need to do in order to make the money, which is making wise investments.

Investments are the things that will comprise either your assets or your liabilities. Surely, getting rich requires you to make these investments an asset instead of liability. You need every investment to add some value to your wealth, even if only indirectly. But how can you exactly do that?

Making wise choices when it comes to investments is a must. Not only should you make utmost research and rigorous planning, you should likewise have perfect execution.

Here are some of the things you need to do in order to make a wise investment:

- Invest in things you know of

The most fundamental step in making a wise investment is to invest in things which you personally know of. As much as possible, you must be an expert in the field you are entering. Remember that you cannot just venture in the unknown and expect it to go your way. Your hard-earned money need not depend on pure luck!

Just imagine, how can you deal with problematic situations regarding your investment if you don't know anything about it? As an investor, you have to make the crucial steps in taking your investment forward which would be almost impossible without any knowledge at all about such investment. On the contrary, knowing your way around an investment is almost half the battle won.

- Consider the trend

Sometimes, the trend dictates whether or not you are making a good investment. While it is okay to have classic investments, it is also advisable to go along with the trend once in a while. Know which era you are in and play around it. After all, people also change in order to accommodate the trends, so must you. Your investments should be dynamic enough to go with the trends yet strong enough to withstand trend changes.

- Take risks once in a while

While it is normal for investors to go safe for the sake of their hard-earned capital, it is also advisable to take risks once in a while. Remember that taking risks helps you become a wiser investor in the long run. It is only through taking risks that you will truly understand its nature and consequences, so taking risks is actually a learning experience that you should undergo.

- Do not put all your money in a single investment

As the famous saying advice goes, 'do not put all your eggs in one basket'. This advice take into account risks associated with putting all your assets/money in a single investment. This is the logical solution if you want to protect your assets from a major meltdown.

Putting your money in a single investment makes it more vulnerable to breakdown. If you have just one investment, your fortune will depend solely on such. If that single investment fails, everything you have put into it will be lost and you will have nothing left. On the contrary, if you put your money in different investments, your whole fortune cannot be easily shattered by the fall of one. This also gives you the option to expand your market and enter another industry. Whatever it is, make sure that your money is not put in a single investment.

- Think about the exchange

Decision-making is a very crucial skill that one has to master if they were to succeed in making investments; and surely, there would be times when you would have to make these important financial decisions. One of the things that you have to consider during these times is the exchange – what does that mean?

There are always two sides in an investment: 1) the thing you will let go; and 2) the thing that you will get. Having an investment means that you are definitely letting go of money – but the more crucial question is, what will you get out of it? This is called the exchange.

If you're going to pull out money from your pocket to make an investment, make sure that you are getting more in return. Don't invest in things which would likely give you lesser or same returns, because that would surely not make you rich. Always aim for an exchange where you are at an advantage.

Of course, there will be risks associated with your investments. But you see, you have to calculate the risks properly in order to know whether you are on the winning end or not. If you think you'll be in the losing end, the right thing to do would be obvious – drop it.

In every investment you make, be sure that you study carefully the exchange that will follow. The lesson: weigh everything in your favor.

Chapter 3 - Buy Your Own House

It wouldn't be very surprising to know that those who rent an apartment are one step farther to being rich than those who own their own house. The sad thing is that, these people might not even know why that is. They just keep on falling in the cycle of paying for their rents, and being dragged down from financial success. Below are the reasons why you should buy your own house instead of renting out your place:

- Rent is a lifetime expense

Rent is a lifetime expense because you would have to pay for it as long as you live, just like food, water and clothing. This does not have to be that way if you would have your own house to retire in. If you have your own house, you won't have to deal with lifetime expense, except for maintenance. This is like taking one worry out of your list! Moreover, having this lifetime expense prevents you from saving money that you could otherwise use as a capital for worthy investments.

- Renting a house gives very little security

Just the thought that your landowner would oust you anytime already makes you restless about the future. Since you wouldn't have any claim over the house, you would feel unstable for the most part of your stay as opposed to having the security of living in your own house.

- Renting a house is a senseless waste of money

Remember the discussion about exchange? Renting a house is the perfect example of not getting an equal exchange. When you rent a house, you get only a temporary convenience of having a place to stay in. Is that really worth a lifetime expense? Surely, the answer is no! Just imagine spending millions on a thing which you cannot even claim ownership over.

To be rich, you have to get rid of these worries! Find a place you can call your home and at the same time, your own!

Chapter 4 - Get Insured

Accidents happen day in and day out. It can happen to all people and truth be told, even you wouldn't be able to tell when it would happen to you. It is an inevitable force of life no one can escape.

But while it is inevitable, you don't have to feel helpless about it! The least that you can do is be prepared to face these untoward events head on. But how exactly can you do that? The answer is simple – be insured.

Getting insurance seems like a wise option today, with all the dangers and calamities that seem to escalate every year. While it may look like an unwelcome expense for you, it could actually be your saving grace in times of need.

Availing of insurance is a must precaution if you want to be rich. It prevents you from losing everything that you have worked hard for by reason of an unfortunate event. It minimizes the risk associated with the extraordinary events of life at a very little cost. Most importantly, it gives you the peace of mind when it comes to your properties, to your health, and to your life.

For a basic coverage, you should avail of the following insurance:

- Health insurance
- Fire Insurance
- Calamity Insurance
- Life Insurance

Chapter 5 - Manage Your Spending

Your spending is as important as your income generating activities. Being rich does not depend solely on your ability to make income, it is also dependent on your ability to control your expenses. Remember that what goes in (the income) can be offset by what goes out (expenses), in which case you can say that you haven't really earned one bit. Worse, uncontrollable spending may even lead to losses and debts, if it goes more the allowable limit for your spending which is 80% of your income (as discussed in chapter 1).

If you want to be rich, you have to know this basic rule: spend wisely.

The good news is that being rich does not prevent you from spending at all; it only means that you have to be wise as you spend. The next question now would be, how could you be a wise spender? Here are the tips:

- Segregate what you need and what you want

Some people mistake what they want for what they need and spend more as a result. When you have a limited budget, always prioritize to buy the things you need because these are the things that you need to have come what may. If you buy the things you want first, you will end up having less money for your needs. Since these are your needs, you become compelled to buy them thus the resort to your savings, if any.

On the contrary, buying what you need first will allow you to have what you need and choose which among your fixations can be bought without the guilt if there is spare money.

- Go for multi-functional items

Buying one thing that could serve several purposes can definitely be considered as a good buy. Always look for these multi-functional items and save more!

- Don't give in to impulse buying

There will always be temptations along the way, but you don't have to give in to them! These temptations will always urge you to go on impulse buying that would have you spending more than you should. The key to avoiding impulse buying is to always carry a list of the things you need to buy with you as you shop. More importantly, don't just carry the list but stick to it!

Remember that being rich and being a wise spender goes hand in hand with one another, so you'd better practice wise spending now!

Chapter 6 - Attracting Money: Explore All Ways Of Generating Income

The last thing that you should know about being rich is attracting money which could only be by exploring all the ways of generating income. Remember that the previous chapters would be useless if you would not work hard to generate income under your name. The world is full of surprises and more often than not, it would not give you the riches on your first attempt. This does not mean you should give up! It only means that you have to try again and explore all the ways available to you.

As a basic rule, you need to have two types of income which are active and passive income. Active income is that you get from actively participating in its generation such as compensation and business income. In other words, this is what you get by working hard. On the other hand, passive income is the one you get without actively participating in its generation such as interest, dividends and the like.

You must strive to have not only active income, but also passive income. Remember that you cannot work forever and there will come a time that only your passive income will sustain you. Moreover, passive income will allow you to gain without actively participating in it, so you would be able to multiply your earning capacity as a result.

Do not just be complacent in where you are now. Remember that just because you are in good state does not mean that it couldn't get any better. The key to being rich starts with your dreams, so aim high and start building your dream now!

Conclusion

Thank you again for purchasing this book on creating and keeping wealth like the rich. I hope this book was able to help you to unravel some of the mysteries behind wealth creation and begin to use these principles to build your own financial fortress.

I am extremely excited to pass this information along to you, and I am so happy that you now have read and can hopefully implement these strategies going forward.

If you are lucky enough to have already amassed great wealth I applaud you and thank you for taking the time to read this book. Hopefully you were still able to find some way in which this book could add value to your life. If you know of anyone else that could benefit from the information presented here please alert them of this book.

Finally, if you enjoyed this book and feel that it has enlightened you in any way, please take the time to share your thoughts and post a review on Amazon. It'd be greatly appreciated!

Thank you and good luck!

Preview Of:

Hot Small Business Ideas

25 Smokin' Hot Business Ideas For Success

Introduction

I want to thank you and congratulate you for purchasing the book, *"Hot Small Business Ideas - 25 Smokin' Hot Business Ideas For Success"*.

This book contains 25 proven small business ideas to find the right niche for you to become successful.

Congratulations on making the first step towards a better life for yourself and your loved ones. Creating a business is the financially smartest thing you can do in today's often volatile job market. As more and more folks get laid off in the rapidly changing economy we live in, more and more people are looking for a more stable source of income in which they have better control of.

I could go on and on about the benefits of owning and operating your own business, but I won't because that's not why you are here. You already know you want to own your own business and make your own decisions, you just need to know where to channel your drive and hard work. In this book you will find 25 of the Hottest Small Business Ideas for today!

One thing I have learned over the years of being an entrepreneur is that if you don't have passion for the business you are in - then you most likely will not make it. I'm here to fuel that passion by giving you some great ideas you can really sink your teeth into.

Thanks again for purchasing this book, I hope you enjoy it!

Chapter 1: Starting Your Own Online Business

Nobody gets rich by remaining an employee forever. You need to take greater risks, invest and be your own boss to earn more and provide a much better life for yourself and your family. That is practically how your bosses does it.

There is no better time to start a small business than now. Marketing has never been easier, thanks to the multitude of channels, tools and online facilities that help you have success in marketing without spending a dime. The awareness in business management is also higher, so you will have more time and opportunities to thrive in your chosen industry and make a name for yourself.

Starting your own business is not just about the extra income; it is about the extra time for yourself and your family, and all the comfortable and luxurious perks that come with it. Starting your own smoking hot business is your ultimate ticket to better living, having all resources to buy whatever you want and plan ahead without having to consider vacation/leave credits, office schedules and unrelenting superiors.

Being your own boss is a life-changing decision that can steer your whole life – upwards if you have the dedication and willingness to learn and develop your craft, or downwards if you cannot commit to your decision.

For a starter, you will be introduced to the hottest online businesses you can possibly start.

1. Amazon Affiliate

Affiliate programs are smoking hot; double that for Amazon. This is the new version of product consignment, only done online. You will need to do the marketing, promotions and reviews preferably in the form of blogging to get more customers for Amazon's listed products. This is a fulltime online business with unlimited earning opportunities.

Pros:

- *Famous* – Amazon is the top online shopping site all around the world. The name sells in itself. The program is reliable and has been around for more than a decade now. It is definitely the most trusted affiliate program today.

- *Flexible time* – All the marketing efforts and website setups are all in your good time. You can keep earning while sleeping, so management is not stressful.

- *Low-cost* – Your only expense is the domain and server, although there are free providers you can choose from.

Cons:

- *Might take time to pick up* – Gaining huge online traffic and website contents may take time, perhaps months before you can actually earn. The good thing is that when it picks up, there is no stopping it.

- *Requires intense internet marketing know-how* – Millions of people all around the world do marketing online. If you want to standout, you need to master the techniques and learn continuously.

2. Niche Blogging

Blogging doesn't run out of steam, and it continues to be the new newspaper, magazine, paperback, diary and variety show. According to Yahoo, the blogging industry recorded its highest revenue in 2013, and there is no sign of backing down anytime soon. Average niche bloggers earn anywhere from $1,000 to $15,000 a month, the latter implying the full-timers.

Pros:

- *Unlimited source of income* – You can earn from ad vendors, paid advertising, PPC, paid publicity and promotions, affiliate programs and dozens more of innovative online opportunities.

- *Easy to set up* – You only need to have flair in writing – informing and entertaining at the same time. Setting up your blog is easy and in fact, you can have it for free. Just pick a topic and niche market you want to tap, and be the best in it.

Cons:

- *Traffic problems* – Online traffic can be a big problem if you will only focus on the actual blogging part. Remember that this is a business; thus, it involves intense marketing and customer relations.

- *Requires patience* – You can't write and have thousands of readers right away. Even the most successful bloggers today needed to build their fan-base over time.

3. SEO Firm

SEO (search engine optimization) is the life of websites, both non-profit and commercial. SEO dictates the competition. It doesn't run out of market.

Your business' goal here is to get clients on top of search engines and get them the traffic and conversion that they are targeting. If you have advance knowledge in web and graphic designing, SEO writing, SEM (search engine marketing) and internet marketing strategies, you are ready to get some clients and build websites for them. A team of five specialists is already enough to handle a pool of business websites.

Pros:

- *Easy to set up* – What you do when you make your own website or blog is the same thing you will do for your clients. You might just need support staff for the other technical aspects and to finish projects on deadlines.

- *Low-cost* – Most likely, you already have a usable computer. You only need to buy different software (you can get them for free if you are adept in online sourcing) and additional computers – perhaps rent a server.

- *Easy to market* – Your body of work speaks for itself. The market is unlimited, and your efficiency in the job will dictate how far you can get in the industry.

Cons:

- *Tough competition* – At the end of the day, your client's online success (in terms of traffic generation, search engine ranking, etc.) will gauge your reputation. There is only one page to aim at but, there are thousands of websites competing. The competition is not only between you and other SEO firms. You need to remember that your client's stand in the competition is also your responsibility.

4. Graphic Designing

You can launch this business as a part of SEO services for company websites and professional bloggers. However, a graphic designing company can also stand alone as it really was before SEO became the buzz. If you are adept in designing, working on your own shouldn't be a problem at all.

You can cater to bloggers and social media addicts who want to take their accounts to another level (many Facebook-ers and Youtube-ers hire graphic and video designers and editors to professionalize their accounts). You can also cater to special occasions, such as weddings, birthday parties, launchings, etc.

Pros:

- *Wide, unlimited market* – Graphic designing services have been here even before they were integrated with SEO. Specifically, those who hire graphic designers belong to small-scale businesses and private individuals. Your own talent will be your own setback.
- *Low startup cost* – You need a piece of computer, internet connection, printer and a whole lot of creative ingenuity. Depending on the volume of your clientele, you can expand in resources as you expand in operation.

Cons:

- *Professionally limiting* – Many experts believe that graphic designing should just be the beginning of a more expansive business because this alone is very limiting, professional at least. There's not exactly a next level, unless you include other services and provide tangible products as well, such as selling your own souvenir items or expanding to other SEO services as well.

5. eBook Self-Publication

Book and eBook writing are both professions, but self-publication of eBooks is a business. It involves end-to-end processes, from the writing to editing, cover designing to online publication, and marketing to selling. Many bloggers have already shifted to fulltime eBook self-publication as the potential income is higher.

Amazon and Barnes and Noble are the two top online destinations when it comes to eBook publication. You will likely receive just a percentage of the eBook price, but the accumulated earnings are enough to top your monthly income from a fulltime office job. Selling through your own website is also a lucrative idea, but only if you attract huge online traffic and has already set yourself as one of the leaders in your niche industry.

Pros:

- *Unlimited earning potential* – As of 2012, eBook sales have already surpassed hardcover sales, but only next to paperback sales. In the next five to 10 years, it is expected that online publication will be the most marketable form of publication.

- *A potential launch pad to stardom* – This business is not only about the money – millions of money. It is also about legacy, name and popularity.

- *Easy to execute* – Writing shouldn't be a problem. Most of your efforts will go to the cover design and marketing strategies.

Cons:

- *Needs decent online presence* – If you will market your own eBooks, you need to have an existing market-base. Otherwise, starting from scratch will take time to convert into sales.

- *Possible failure* – The failure in the self-publication industry is really high. Many eBook writers don't even crack the 200-sales threshold. If you think your writing skills and creativity are not enough to make a name for yourself, better choose another business.

6. eBay Trading

eBay is the best channel to start a trading business because all types of products are allowed, both new and used. The site is famous for its cheap finds, so pulling a chunk of the market should not be a problem.

You can source out your products from wholesalers, abroad, garage sales, or you can restore old items to make them new.

Pros:

- *High traffic volume* – Six out of 10 internet users have bought an item from eBay. That is how often eBay makes a sales, which means that market is far from being saturated anytime soon.

- *Easy to set up* – When you already have products to sell, you only need a camera, computer and basic knowledge in setting up an eBay account. You can do your own internet marketing, but eBay is already an established shopping destination. Customers go to the site without prodding.

- *Low startup cost* – Depending on your items, your capital can be as low as a couple of hundreds of dollars. It doesn't matter if you sell second-hand items.

Cons:

- *Difficulty with logistics* – This shouldn't really be a problem because dealing with forwarding and logistic company, both local and international, is now simpler.

Nonetheless, you need to take care of it as well, which means extra work.

7. Content Creating

Others call it SEO and technical writing, but content writing is more than just a single component of a fulltime SEO firm. Content writing is less focused on internet marketing stuff – just plain quality content. In the 90s, content writing referred to the outsourced company magazine contents, that included internal newsletters, free magazine giveaways (as a part of store promos) and local ads. Today, content writing primarily refers to website and blog writing, mostly of private organizations that use their websites not as primary marketing channels but as information centers (which is true for most consumer products that do not really sell online).

Pros:

- *High expected revenue* – Yahoo considers content writing as one of the biggest profession for the next 50 years, especially now that everything is shifting to online publication. The revenue and market are likely to expand without stopping.

- *Simple organizational structure* – A small content writing business doesn't even need to have an office. Most similar companies pool writers online and have them work in virtual offices. You can even do it by yourself if you will take one client at a time.

Cons:

- *Quality concerns* – For a bigger clientele, quality control might be a problem, especially when you do not have in-house editors to help you do quality control, proofreading and copyediting.

8. Server Management

Buying a dedicated server is not something that many small businesses can afford or are even willing to invest in. Server management companies then buy a server space and have it leased out to small companies. You can also have your own server and have it rented as shared server to several clients.

In addition, you must offer support and website management services.

Pros:

- *Huge ROI* – Leasing out a server alone may not incur impressive income, but because of the additional services, you can place a huge premium on top.

- *Huge market-base* – This is a very timely business, so relevant in today's business environment that will not run out of prospective clients in the next few years.

Cons:

- *Requires technical expertise* – Basic knowledge in server management is not enough. You need to have advance skills to make sure that your services are on top.

- *Limited clients* – The size of your clientele will depend on the size of your server.

Thanks for Previewing My Exciting Book Entitled:

"Small Business: Hot Small Business Ideas!"

To purchase this book, simply go to the Amazon Kindle store and simply search:

"SMALL BUSINESS"

Then just scroll down until you see my book. You will know it is mine because you will see my name "James Harper" underneath the title.

Alternatively, you can visit my author page on Amazon to see this book and other work I have done. Thanks so much, and please don't forget your free bonuses

DON'T LEAVE YET! - YOUR FREE BONUSES ARE BELOW!

Free Bonus Offer 1: Get Free Access To The OperationAwesomeLife.com VIP Newsletter!

Free Bonus Offer 2: Get A Free Download Of My Friends Amazing Book "Passive Income" First Chapter!

Free Bonus Offer 3: Get A Free Email Series On Making Money Online When You Join Newsletter!

GET ALL 3 FREE

Once you enter your email address you will immediately get free access to this awesome **VIP NEWSLETTER**!

For a limited time, if you join for free right now, you will also get free access to the first chapter of the awesome book "**PASSIVE INCOME**"!

And, last but definitely not least, if you join the newsletter right now, you also will get a free 10 part email series on **10 SUCCESS SECRETS OF MAKING MONEY ONLINE!**

To claim all 3 of your FREE BONUSES just click below!

Just Go Here for all 3 VIP bonuses!

OperationAwesomeLife.com